reflections *on wildness*

# reflections
## *on wildness*

WINDHORSE PUBLICATIONS

Published by Windhorse Publications
11 Park Road
Birmingham
B13 8AB
www.windhorsepublications.com

Cover photo Devamitra
Design Marlene Eltschig
Printed by Interprint Ltd, Marsa, Malta

A catalogue record for this book is available
from the British Library


ISBN 1 899579 34 6

contents

1   Introduction
7   Sojourns in the Parallel World
9   The Darkness comes Rattling
10   Song of the Open Road
12   The Wildwood Delights
16   Forest Path
17   Wind
19   'I want to break out ...'
20   A Refuge and a Sanctuary
22   The Desire to Fly
24   The Work of the Forest
26   The desert has many teachings
27   The Dakini
30   To be a Slave of Intensity
32   The Disappearance of Wildness
33   The Panther
34   The Jaguar
36   The Tyger
38   The Wild Horse of the Mind
40   The Collar
42   Why am I so lost?
45   The Buddha in the Forest
47   Princess Mandarava goes forth
52   Yeshe Tsogyal and the Wild Beasts
55   The Wild Swans at Coole
57   Owls
58   Inversnaid
59   Our Limits Transgressed
60   Peace in the Wilderness
61   Life in the Forest

# INTRODUCTION

This collection was inspired by the efforts of some friends of mine to create a retreat centre, a place where women may prepare themselves for ordination in a Western Buddhist context. The search is on for somewhere wild and remote, a place far from the calls of domestic and professional life where – at least for a while – women can attend to 'what really matters', as Longchenpa, one of the writers in this collection, would say.

My friends have called their project 'Aranya'. This Sanskrit word refers to a place, or state of mind, 'beyond the village' – beyond the safe and secure, the humdrum and everyday. The aranya might be a forest or cave dwelling, or anywhere remote. It is somewhere that is peaceful – and also wild....

This book is offered in support of Aranya – to help with the funding and also to consider the nature, the ethos, of the project. After all, what is aranya, what is wildness?

This collection offers, in its own way, some suggestions.

In a way, reflecting on wildness seems a contradiction in terms. The intentionally reflective nature of this anthology means that there is nothing frenetic here: this is not about having a wild time in the partying sense. It was impossible to resist including a Buddhist story about a young man who is supposed to be meditating in the forest, but is distracted by the sounds of a party happening in the nearby village.

Much closer to the spirit of reflection is the wildness of nature, and this is represented here in many ways – in fact, a veritable jungle of wild animals seems to have prowled into the collection. Many of our writers dwell on the sheer beauty and peace of being in the wilderness, as compared to the stress of city life – reflections that seem poignant in a world in which wild places are fast disappearing. In other extracts, though, we get a sense of the challenges and terrors of life in the wilds, and the courage needed to overcome that fear.

As well as the beautiful and awe-inspiring wildness to be found in the world around us, there is another kind: the wildness within. In this collection we find Walt Whitman exulting in the freedom and spaciousness of life 'loos'd of limits and imaginary lines'. On the other hand, the Buddhist tradition often speaks of taming the mind, calming the turbulence within us, and a number of the writings here reflect this; Milarepa, for example, speaks of the wild horse of the mind, whose bridle is 'ever-flowing inspiration'. And one of the arguably more idiosyncratic selections is 'The Collar', by George Herbert, which seems to say so much about the struggle that taming one's rebellious mind inevitably sometimes is.

I have found it fascinating to reflect on the relationship between the outer wilderness, the deserts and forests that are the traditional domain of meditators, and the inner calm that such places evoke. I am glad to dedicate this book to the attempt to explore that relationship which the Aranya project represents, to the women who are bringing it into being, and to all those women whose lives will be touched by it. I am very grateful to everyone who has worked on the book, and especially Padmavajri, who has handled it with her customary grace.

Vidyadevi

# SOJOURNS
# IN THE PARALLEL WORLD

We live our lives of human passions,
cruelties, dreams, concepts,
crimes and the exercise of virtue
in and beside a world devoid
of our preoccupations, free
from apprehension – though affected,
certainly, by our actions. A world
parallel to our own, though overlapping.
We call it 'Nature'; only reluctantly
admitting ourselves to be 'Nature' too.
Whenever we lose track of our own
    obsessions,
our self-concerns, because we drift for
    a minute,
an hour even, of pure (almost pure)
response to that insouciant life:
cloud, bird, fox, the flow of light, the
    dancing
pilgrimage of water, vast stillness
of spellbound ephemerae on a lit
    windowpane,
animal voices, mineral hum, wind

conversing with rain, ocean with rock,
   stuttering
of fire to coal – then something tethered
in us, hobbled like a donkey on its patch
of gnawed grass and thistles, breaks free.
No one discovers
just where we've been, when we're caught
   up again
into our own sphere (where we must
return, indeed, to evolve our destinies)
– but we have changed, a little.

Denise Levertov

# THE DARKNESS COMES RATTLING

How shall I begin my song
In the blue night that is settling?

In the great night my heart will go out,
Toward me the darkness comes rattling.
In the great night my heart will go out.

Owl Woman

# SONG OF THE OPEN ROAD

From this hour I ordain myself loos'd of
    limits and imaginary lines,
Going where I list, my own master total
    and absolute,
Listening to others, considering well what
    they say,
Pausing, searching, receiving,
    contemplating,
Gently, but with undeniable will, divesting
    myself of the holds that would hold me.

I inhale great draughts of space,
The east and the west are mine, and the
    north and the south are mine.

I am larger, better than I thought,
I did not know I held so much goodness.

All seems beautiful to me,
I can repeat over to men and women You
    have done such good to me I would do
    the same to you,

I will recruit for myself and you as I go,
I will scatter myself among men and
    women as I go,
I will toss a new gladness and roughness
    among them,
Whoever denies me it shall not trouble me,
Whoever accepts me he or she shall be
    blessed and shall bless me.

Walt Whitman
*'Song of the Open Road'*

# THE WILDWOOD DELIGHTS

Well, my dear mind, listen to the charms
   of the wildwood:
Precious trees, ready to honor the
   Victorious Ones and
Heavy with fruits, grow splendidly in
   the wildwood,
(With) leaves and fragrant flowers that
   are wide open and
(Graced by) the sweet smell of incense and
   the balminess of a light breeze.

Its waist, on which the drum-beat of
   waterfalls resounds melodiously and
   which is
Bathed in the cool light of the moon,
Is covered by a garment of thick clouds and
In them the crowd of stars adds to the
   encompassing beauty.

Flocks of geese swim on sweet-smelling
   ponds and
Many birds and deer move happily about;

Among lotus flowers and wish-granting
   trees and water lilies,
Bees flit and hum their songs.

Trees seem by their swaying (in the wind)
   to perform a dance, and by
Bending their branches with creepers as the
   tips of their fingers
To invite the guest, saying: 'Please come.'

Cool and clear rivulets blanketed
   by lotus flowers
Seem to be the bright splendor of
   a smiling face.

Wearing diadems of garden flowers and
   evergreens, and
Holding tightly to the azure sky as their
   garments,
The gods, resembling stars in the bright sky,
Seem to shower amorous attentions
   (on each other) in this pleasure grove.

While the cuckoo sings its drunken,
    piercing song
The flowers seem to be buoyed up by the
    cool seasonal wind.

While the cloud-elephants are trumpeting
    their joy
The coming of the rainy season seems to
    pour forth its abundant beneficence.

Roots, leaves, and edible fruits
Are unpolluted in the wildwood and
    available in all four seasons.

Since none is there to speak unpleasant
    words,
In the wildwood emotional outbursts
    decrease;
Since you are far removed from the turmoil
    of the cities,
In the wildwood steady thoughts of
    calmness grow.

Being in harmony with life's true meaning,
   the mind becomes meek and
Comes close to the bliss of inner peace in
   the wildwood.

In brief, the charms of the wildwood are
   unlimited;
Even if you were to talk for aeons, how
   could you ever exhaust (their abundance)?

*from 'The Story of the Wildwood Delights'*
*in Longchenpa's 'A Visionary Journey'*
trans. Herbert V. Guenther

# FOREST PATH

A moment when, suddenly,
looking back for the way to the future,
you quiver on the edge of yourself.

– All paths panic beneath you,
the motherlode of meaning splits,
gusts east in grits;
the sun throws unmanageable glances
blinding off the choppy water
and spray plumes off, twisting, into empty
  blue.

And you turn, to find yourself
on the winding forest path.
Yes, a violet poses against a leaf
and alarmed wrens flitter in birches.
Now you cling breathless onto
a few memories, a mug of tea,
but you know they are not your home.

Thomas Jones

16

# WIND

This house has been far out at sea all night,
The woods crashing through darkness, the
   booming hills,
Winds stampeding the fields under the
   window
Floundering black astride and blinding wet

Till day rose; then under an orange sky
The hills had new places, and wind wielded
Blade-light, luminous black and emerald,
Flexing like the lens of a mad eye.

At noon I scaled along the house-side as far as
The coal-house door. Once I looked up –
Through the brunt wind that dented the
   balls of my eyes
The tent of the hills drummed and strained
   its guyrope,

The fields quivering, the skyline a grimace,
At any second to bang and vanish with
   a flap:

The wind flung a magpie away and
   a black-
Back gull bent like an iron bar slowly. The
   house

Rang like some fine green goblet in the
   note
That any second would shatter it. Now
   deep
In chairs, in front of the great fire, we grip
Our hearts and cannot entertain book,
   thought,

Or each other. We watch the fire blazing,
And feel the roots of the house move, but
   sit on,
Seeing the window tremble to come in,
Hearing the stones cry out under the
   horizons.

Ted Hughes

## 'I WANT TO BREAK OUT ...'

I want to break out,
Batter down the door,
Go tramping black heather all day
On the windy moor,
And at night, in hayloft, or under hedge,
    find
A companion suited to my mind.

I want to break through,
Shatter time and space,
Cut up the Void with a knife,
Pitch the stars from their place,
Nor shrink back when, lidded with
    darkness, the Eye
Of Reality opens and blinds me, blue as
    the sky.

Sangharakshita

# A REFUGE AND A SANCTUARY

*B*lasts from the Channel, with raining scud, and spume of mist breaking upon the hills, have kept me indoors all day. Yet not for a moment have I been dull or idle, and now, by the latter end of a sea-coal fire, I feel such enjoyment of my ease and tranquillity that I must needs word it before going up to bed.

Of course one ought to be able to breast weather such as this of to-day, and to find one's pleasure in the strife with it. For the man sound in body and serene of mind there is no such thing as bad weather; every sky has its beauty, and storms which whip the blood do but make it pulse more vigorously. I remember the time when I would have set out with gusto for a tramp along the wind-swept and rain-beaten roads; nowadays, I should perhaps pay for the experiment with my life. All the more do I prize the shelter of these good walls, the honest workmanship which makes my doors and windows proof against the assailing blast. In all England, the land of comfort, there is no room more comfortable than this in which I sit. Comfortable in the good old sense of the word, giving solace to the mind no less than ease to the body. And never does it look more homely, more a refuge and a sanctuary, than on winter nights.

George Gissing
*The Private Papers of Henry Ryecroft*

21

# THE DESIRE TO FLY

*I*t was furthest from the house of all the trees, on a waste weedy spot which no one else visited, and this made it an ideal place for me, and whenever I was in the wild arboreal mood I would climb the willow to find a good stout branch high up on which to spend an hour, with a good view of the wide green plain before me and the sight of grazing flocks and herds, and of houses and poplar groves looking blue in the distance. Here, too, in this tree I first felt the desire for wings, to dream of the delight it would be to circle upwards to a great height and float on the air without effort, like the gull and buzzard and harrier and other great soaring land and water birds. But from the time this notion and desire began to affect me I envied most the great crested screamer, an inhabitant then of all the marshes in our vicinity. For here was a bird as big or bigger than a goose, as heavy almost as I was myself, who, when he wished to fly, rose off the ground with tremendous labour, and then as he got higher and higher and flew more and more easily, until he rose so high that he looked no bigger than a lark or pipit, and at that height he would continue floating round and round in vast circles for hours, pouring out those jubilant cries at intervals which sounded to us so far below like clarion notes in the sky. If I could only get off the ground like that heavy bird and rise as high, then the blue air would make me as buoyant and let me float all day without pain or effort like the bird! This desire has continued with me through my life, yet I have never wished to fly in a balloon or airship, since I should then be tied to a machine and have no will or soul of my own. The desire has only been gratified a very few times in that kind of dream called levitation, when one rises and floats above the earth without effort and is like a ball of thistle-down carried by the wind.

W.H. Hudson
*Far Away and Long Ago*

# THE WORK OF THE FOREST

The Buddha was staying among the Kosalan people in a certain forest thicket, in which, it so happened, the brahmin Navakammika Bharadvaja was working. When he saw the Blessed One sitting cross-legged in the shade of a sal tree, upright, with mindfulness clearly established, the brahmin thought: 'I'm enjoying my work here in the forest. But what is that meditator enjoying?'

So Navakammika came closer to the Buddha and said:

Wanderer, what work are you doing
    here among the sal trees?
    Alone in the forest,
    what gives you delight?

And the Blessed One said:

There is no work left for me to do in the
    forest.
    All the tangles are completely sorted out.
    I am free from all briars
    and, my heart unpierced,
    I delight in being alone,
    all discontent completely gone.

*Navakammika Sutta*
*Samyutta-Nikaya VII.17*

# THE DESERT
# HAS MANY TEACHINGS

In the desert,
Turn toward emptiness,
Fleeing the self.

Stand alone,
Ask no one's help,
And your being will quiet,
Free from the bondage of things.

Those who cling to the world
endeavor to free them;
Those who are free, praise.

Care for the sick,
But live alone,
Happy to drink from the waters of sorrow,
To kindle Love's fire
With the twigs of a simple life.

Thus you will live in the desert.

Mechtild of Magdeburg

# THE DAKINI

The groundedness of interconnectedness together with the uncompromising challenge of self-transcendence finds symbolic expression in one of the most positive images of women's evolution known to humankind. In a pantheon of female Buddhas, gods and goddesses, and a host of enlightening beings, we discover the dakini of ancient Tantric Buddhism. The dakini, or sky dancer, expresses a passionate commitment to the truth and symbolizes the transformative energy of the transcendental in female form.

The word 'dakini' comes from a Sanskrit root meaning direction, space, or sky. Dakini is usually translated as sky walker, or sky dancer. The sky symbolizes the open dimension of being, an infinite space in which there is complete freedom of movement. The dakini dances in this open space, enjoying complete spiritual liberation. Her body is naked, symbolizing her uncompromising commitment to truth; nothing about her is veiled or hidden or held back. She may take on any hue of the rainbow, but she is usually depicted as red. Red, the colour of blood, signals the great upsurge of emotional energy that floods through her entire being, and flushes her whole body a bright crimson. She is ornamented with human bones that clatter against each other as she moves. Her long black hair is wild and dishevelled – she cares nothing for appearances. Conventional notions of propriety don't touch her. She is concerned, above all, with direct experience of reality, and a passionate commitment to fully meeting that. As she dances through the sky, she cries out in a deep laugh of utter freedom.

Western women who come into contact with this image of the dakini are very attracted to it. Perhaps this is because of the unrestrained flow of her energy. She is a far cry from the ever-meek and holy Virgin Mary with her downcast eyes, and a real relief from that whited sepulchre known as the Angel in the House. The dakini enjoys life to the full, and refuses to compromise her passionate pursuit of the truth.

Sinhadevi

# TO BE A SLAVE OF INTENSITY

Friend, hope for the Guest while you are
  alive.
Jump into experience while you are alive!
Think ... and think ... while you are alive.
What you call 'salvation' belongs to the
  time before death.

If you don't break your ropes while you're
  alive,
do you think
ghosts will do it after?

The idea that the soul will join with the
  ecstatic
just because the body is rotten —
that is all fantasy.
What is found now is found then.
If you find nothing now,
you will simply end up with an apartment
  in the City of Death.

If you make love with the divine now, in
   the next life you will have the face of
   satisfied desire.

So plunge into the truth, find out who the
   Teacher is, Believe in the Great Sound!

Kabir says this: When the Guest is being
searched for, it is the intensity of the
longing for the Guest that does all the
work.
Look at me, and you will see a slave of that
intensity.

*Kabir*
trans. Robert Bly

# THE DISAPPEARANCE OF WILDNESS

Wildness and silence disappeared from the countryside, sweetness fell from the air, not because anyone wished them to vanish or fall but because throughways had to floor the meadows with cement to carry the automobiles which advancing technology produced.... Tropical beaches turned into high-priced slums where thousand-room hotels elbowed each other for glimpses of once-famous surf not because those who loved the beaches wanted them there but because enormous jets could bring a million tourists every year – and therefore did.

Archibald MacLeish
*'The Great American Frustration'*,
*in 'Saturday Review', New York, 9 July 1968*

# THE PANTHER

*In the Jardin des Plantes, Paris*

His vision, from the constantly passing bars,
has grown so weary that it cannot hold
anything else. It seems to him there are
a thousand bars; and behind the bars, no
   world.

As he paces in cramped circles, over and
   over,
the movement of his powerful soft strides
is like a ritual dance around a center
in which a mighty will stands paralyzed,

Only at times, the curtain of the pupils
lifts, quietly − . An image enters in,
rushes down through the tensed, arrested
   muscles,
plunges into the heart and is gone.

Rainer Maria Rilke
trans. Stephen Mitchell

# THE JAGUAR

The apes yawn and adore their fleas in the
    sun.
The parrots shriek as if they were on fire,
    or strut
Like cheap tarts to attract the stroller with
    the nut.
Fatigued with indolence, tiger and lion

Lie still as the sun. The boa-constrictor's
    coil
Is a fossil. Cage after cage seems empty, or
Stinks of sleepers from the breathing straw.
It might be painted on a nursery wall.

But who runs like the rest past these arrives
At a cage where the crowd stands, stares,
    mesmerized,
As a child at a dream, at a jaguar hurrying
    enraged
Through prison darkness after the drills of
    his eyes

On a short fierce fuse. Not in boredom –
The eye satisfied to be blind in fire,
By the bang of blood in the brain deaf the
   ear –
He spins from the bars, but there's no cage
   to him

More than to the visionary his cell:
His stride is wildernesses of freedom:
The world rolls under the long thrust of his
   heel.
Over the cage floor the horizons come.

Ted Hughes

# THE TYGER

Tyger Tyger, burning bright,
In the forests of the night;
What immortal hand or eye,
Could frame thy fearful symmetry?

In what distant deeps or skies
Burnt the fire of thine eyes?
On what wings dare he aspire?
What the hand, dare seize the fire?

And what shoulder, and what art,
Could twist the sinews of thy heart?
And when thy heart began to beat,
What dread hand? and what dread feet?

What the hammer? what the chain,
In what furnace was thy brain?
What the anvil? what dread grasp,
Dare its deadly terrors clasp?

When the stars threw down their spears
And water'd heaven with their tears:

Did he smile his work to see?
Did he who made the Lamb make thee?

Tyger Tyger burning bright,
In the forests of the night:
What immortal hand or eye,
Dare frame thy fearful symmetry?

William Blake
*'The Tyger'*
*from 'Songs of Innocence and Experience'*

# THE WILD HORSE OF THE MIND

A horse of Prana-Mind have I;
I adorn him with the silk scarf of Dhyana.
His skin is the magic Ensuing Dhyana
    Stage,
His saddle, illuminating Self-Awareness.
My spurs are the Three Visualizations,
His crupper the secret teaching of the Two
    Gates.

His headstall is the Prana of Vital-force;
His forelock curl is Three-pointed Time.
Tranquillity within is his adornment,
Bodily movement is his rein,
And ever-flowing inspiration is his bridle.

He gallops wildly along the Spine's Central
    Path.
He is a yogi's horse, this steed of mine.

By riding him, one escapes Samsara's mud,
By following him one reaches the safe land
   of Bodhi.

*'The Meeting at Silver Spring'*
*in 'The Hundred Thousand Songs of Milarepa'*

# THE COLLAR

I struck the board, and cry'd, No more.
  I will abroad.
  What? shall I ever sigh and pine?
My lines and life are free; free as the rode,
  Loose as the winde, as large as store.
    Shall I be still in suit?
  Have I no harvest but a thorn
  To let me bloud, and not restore
  What I have lost with cordiall fruit?
    Sure there was wine
Before my sighs did drie it: there was corn
  Before my tears did drown it.
  Is the yeare onely lost to me?
    Have I no bayes to crown it?
No flowers, no garlands gay? all blasted?
      All wasted?
  Not so, my heart: but there is fruit,
    And thou hast hands.
  Recover all thy sigh-blown age
On double pleasures: leave thy cold dispute
Of what is fit, and not. Forsake thy cage,
    Thy rope of sands,

Which pettie thoughts have made, and
    made to thee
    Good cable, to enforce and draw,
            And be thy law,
While thou didst wink and wouldst not
    see.
            Away; take heed:
            I will abroad.
Call in thy deaths head there: tie up thy
    fears.
            He that forbears
        To suit and serve his need,
            Deserves his load.
But as I rav'd and grew more fierce and
    wilde
            At every word,
    Me thought I heard one calling, *Child*!
            And I reply'd, *My Lord*.

George Herbert

# WHY AM I SO LOST?

here shall we go? Where to direct the mind? We have our theories but maybe they are only so much conceit, only cobwebs thrown to catch a leviathan. Does the world offer us any clues? If we watch and listen intently we may be sure that it does. The woodpecker with its on-and-off knocking, the mix of sun and shadow in the woods, the dry beech leaves buzzing in the wind, the busy water carving earth – they all declare the nature of things; they all preach true Dhamma.

Cut off for now from manufactured comforts, wrenched by the turn of seasons, we cannot suppress the upwelling of a question; we cannot keep from blurting to the unconscious river, Why am I so lost? And with the words loosed and blown across the sky like leaves, we find ourselves already drawn on to track down an answer, as if the admission of our ignorance somehow commits us to the search for wisdom.

Reflecting on all this chaotic chance in nature, we see that the instability runs deeper than we imagined, that we who are wondering about the fleeting show are ourselves rushed on like sticks in the flood.

It becomes impossible – as we scan the distances, as we inspect the spinning flotsam, as we review our thoughts – to find anything which does not change and pass away.

We have till now given so little attention to this universal flux that we have failed to understand the laws that work upon us and, being slothful or indifferent or simply careless, we have again and again crashed against huge, frightening questions of pain and longing.

Now, in this wilderness of time, a flood has orphaned us on a strange beach that is itself crumbling into the stream, and wet nature repeats to our senses what we might have learned long before as doctrine: 'All formations are impermanent.' It was one thing to read the words in the quiet of our rooms and another to stand here cold and beleaguered in the midst of unstoppable change.

Bhikkhu Nyanasobhano
*from 'Floodtime'*
*in 'Landscapes of Wonder'*

# THE BUDDHA IN THE FOREST

On such specially auspicious nights as the fourteenth, the fifteenth, and the eighth of the fortnight, I dwelt in such awe-inspiring, horrifying abodes as orchard shrines, woodland shrines, and tree shrines. And while I dwelt there, a wild animal would come up to me, or a peacock would knock off a branch, or the wind would rustle the leaves. I thought: 'What now if this is the fear and dread coming?' I thought: 'Why do I dwell always expecting fear and dread? What if I subdue that fear and dread while keeping the same posture that I am in when it comes upon me?'

While I walked, the fear and dread came upon me; I neither stood nor sat nor lay down till I had subdued that fear and dread. While I stood, the fear and dread came upon me; I neither walked nor sat nor lay down till I had subdued that fear and dread. While I sat, the fear and dread came upon me; I neither walked nor stood nor lay down till

I had subdued that fear and dread. While I lay down, the fear and dread came upon me; I neither walked nor stood nor sat down till I had subdued that fear and dread.

The Buddha
*in the 'Bhayabherava Sutta'*
*Majjhima-Nikaya 4*

## PRINCESS MANDARAVA
## GOES FORTH

The next day, at the crack of dawn, as they all looked on, Mandarava went away without the slightest attachment to the king, her relatives, attendants, wealth, or endowments. She remained, however, in her posture of equipoise, seated within the protective net of Guru Padmasambhava of Oddiyana's loving-kindness and compassion. She traversed not one, but two or three valleys and countries, and suddenly found herself in an uninhabited land that was frightful, wrathful, and rugged beyond belief.

For three long days, she remained trapped in a craggy ravine without food, drink, or shelter. She was famished and chilled to the bone. All she could hear were the eerie sounds of many tropical birds and wild animals. Finally, she managed to climb over a peak, only to find herself forced to descend into yet another frightening valley of doom. Then she lost heart and, in a state of disturbed sorrow, went into the depth of her soul, where her spontaneous, fervent devotion remained unaffected. She cried out in urgent despair: 'Kye ma! Kye hu! Lord Guru of Oddiyana! Guru who reveals the path to liberation! Please look upon me now with your merciful compassion! First, I arrived here in this country to the north. Second, I was engulfed by a dense jungle full of wild animals. Third, the sound of water crashing in craggy ravines is piercing my ears. I fear I am in a barbaric country possessed by demons and cannibals! O young man of grace, where can I find you now? Without you my mind is unstable and weak!

'First, I am here in an uninhabited land where the grass is so wild that the wind makes it dance. Second, there is the unceasing sound of ravens crying in the forest. Third, the sun is obscured by the darkness of night. I wonder if I have entered the bardo between this life and the next? Where is the one whose melodious speech is like music to my ears? That you cannot see me now, at this time, fills my mind with chilling sorrow.

'First, I am alone in this country, without a single companion. Second, it resembles a haunted charnel ground. Third, there is the constant eerie din of jungle creatures. It seems that I have arrived in the city of the lord of death! Be quick to look upon me now with your compassionate mercy! Hold me in your heart, O perfect Lord of Dharma!' Then she fell to the ground in tears.

Through his omniscience, the lotus guru knew of her duress and went to her. Mandarava wept in his presence, so overcome with gratitude that she grabbed him and held him tight. He then spoke these words to her: 'What has become of your fearless pledge of courage now that you are confronted by such a malevolent and unruly land? A frightful environment such as this is the catalyst for a practitioner's true practice to emerge. Adverse conditions are the true wealth of a practitioner. Such a supreme place of practice is the most exalted spot for accomplishing the innermost profound Dharma. A frightening, uncomfortable place is the knife that severs discursive thought. The wrathful charnel ground is the environment through which the deceptive view of eternalism is exposed. To discover the illusory nature of the barren, frightening land is to discover the innermost sacred Dharma. The sound of the jungle is the introduction to the bardo. Sadness and elation, truth and deception – these are non-existent. The true practice of guru devotion is the cultivation of undiminishing fervent faithfulness. This is the resting ground where relief from the bardo is sought. In the bardo the terrifying sounds that resemble a thousand roaring dragons are like the sound of the approaching messengers of the lord of death. Such a storehouse of darkness cannot be illuminated in an aeon of light. It is like being trapped in a thick forest where sharp weapons abound, with the eight terrifying narrow passageways and the four wrathful sounds. The suffering is unbearable beyond imagination!'

Instantly, Mandarava's negativities and obscurations were purified. All the noble qualities that develop on the path arose in her mind.

*from 'The Lives and Liberation*
*of Princess Mandarava'*
trans. Lama Chonam and Sangye Khandro

## YESHE TSOGYAL
## AND THE WILD BEASTS

*T*hen, like a great army converging upon that place, millions upon millions of worms and insects and other crawling things, such as spiders and scorpions and snakes, swarmed over everything. Some of them filled her sense organs; some bit and stung and scratched her as they crawled onto her. Some jumped upon her; others attacked each other, tossing bits of their bodies about as they ate. All sorts of strange and magical forms appeared.

But mTsho-rgyal just trembled a little and felt compassion rise up in her mind. As the forms became more and more angry and frightful, raging around her, mTsho-rgyal thought:

'Many times I have vowed to be unattached to anything associated with body, speech, or mind. All these sentient beings, worms and other crawling things, arise continuously, increasingly, and abundantly from karmic forces. Why should I tremble with fear before such magical manifestations of the elements? I must remember that all activity is the result of good and bad thoughts. Therefore, whatever may arise, either good or bad, I will recognize as dualistic mental activity and be unconcerned.'

Having come to this profound realization, she said:

'All phenomenal existence
is merely the magical manifestation of mind.
I see nothing to fear in all the expanse
    of space.
Therefore, all of this must be self-arising
    luminance.
How could there ever be anything other
    than this?
All these activities are only ornaments of my
    own being.
Better that I rest in meditative silence.'

After saying this, she entered a meditative state that was completely quiet, without any discrimination of good or evil. And all the apparitions disappeared.

Yeshe Tso-gyal
*in 'Mother of Knowledge'*

# THE WILD SWANS AT COOLE

The trees are in their autumn beauty,
The woodland paths are dry,
Under the October twilight the water
Mirrors a still sky;
Upon the brimming water among
   the stones
Are nine-and-fifty swans.

The nineteenth autumn has come upon me
Since I first made my count;
I saw, before I had well finished,
All suddenly mount
And scatter wheeling in great broken rings
Upon their clamorous wings.

I have looked upon those brilliant creatures,
And now my heart is sore.
All's changed since I, hearing at twilight,
The first time on this shore,
The bell-beat of their wings above
   my head,
Trod with a lighter tread.

Unwearied still, lover by lover,
They paddle in the cold
Companionable streams or climb the air;
Their hearts have not grown old;
Passion or conquest, wander where
    they will,
Attend upon them still.

But now they drift on the still water,
Mysterious, beautiful;
Among what rushes will they build,
By what lake's edge or pool
Delight men's eyes when I awake some day
To find they have flown away?

W.B. Yeats

# OWLS

In the night, when the owl is less than exquisitely swift and perfect, the scream of the rabbit is terrible. But the scream of the owl, which is not of pain and hopelessness and the fear of being plucked out of the world, but of the sheer rollicking glory of the death-bringer, is more terrible still. When I hear it resounding through the woods, and then the five black pellets of its song dropping like stones into the air, I know I am standing at the edge of the mystery, in which terror is naturally and abundantly part of life, part of even the most becalmed, intelligent, sunny life – as, for example, my own. The world where the owl is endlessly hungry and endlessly on the hunt is the world in which I live too. There is only one world.

Mary Oliver
'Owls'
from 'Blue Pastures'

# INVERSNAID

This darksome burn, horseback brown,
His rollrock highroad roaring down,
In coop and in comb the fleece of his foam
Flutes and low to the lake falls home.

A windpuff-bonnet of fawn-froth
Turns and twindles over the broth
Of a pool so pitchblack, fell-frowning,
It rounds and rounds Despair to drowning.

Degged with dew, dappled with dew
Are the groins of the braes that the brook
    treads through,
Wiry heathpacks, flitches of fern,
And the beadbonny ash that sits over the burn.

What would the world be, once bereft
Of wet and of wildness? Let them be left,
O let them be left, wildness and wet;
Long live the weeds and the wilderness yet.

Gerard Manley Hopkins

# OUR LIMITS TRANSGRESSED

We can never have enough of Nature. We must be refreshed by the sight of inexhaustible vigor, vast and Titanic features, the sea-coast with its wrecks, the wilderness with its living and its decaying trees, the thunder cloud, and the rain which lasts three weeks and produces freshets. We need to witness our own limits transgressed, and some life pasturing freely where we never wander.

H. Thoreau
*Walden*

# PEACE IN THE WILDERNESS

Standing to one side of him, a deva said to
the Buddha:

These people who dwell in wild places,
living a life so peaceful and simple,
eating just one meal a day,
how is it that they look so serene?

The Buddha said:

They are not sorrowing about the past,
or longing for the future.
They are living in the present.
That's why they look so serene.
It is by sorrowing about the past
and longing for the future
that foolish people wither away,
like green reeds drying in the sun.

Aranna Sutta,
*'The Wilderness'*

## LIFE IN THE FOREST

There was once a wanderer of the Vajjian clan living in the forest near Vesali.

On one occasion there was an all-night party in Vesali, and the noise – the strumming of stringed instruments, the rhythm of drums, and the sound of people talking – was so loud that the wanderer heard it. He started to lament, saying aloud:

Here we all are, each of us quite alone,
living in the forest,
just like a log left lying among the trees.
On a night like this, with a party going on,
who is worse off than us?

It happened that there was a spirit, a deva, living in the same part of the forest.
Upon hearing the wanderer and feeling sympathy for him, the deva decided to bring him to his senses.
So he came close to him and said:

It's true that you're living alone in the forest,
just like a log left lying among the trees.
But many people would envy your life,
just as beings in hell envy those who are
    heaven-bound.

And the wanderer, brought to his senses
by the deva's words, was very moved.

*Vajjiputta Sutta*

acknowledgements

The publishers wish to acknowledge with gratitude permission to quote from the following:

**p.7:** by Denise Levertov, from *Sands of the Well*, copyright © 1996 by Denise Levertov. Reprinted by permission of New Directions Publishing Corp.

**p.12:** *A Visionary Journey* by Longchenpa, translated by Herbert V. Guenther, © 1989 by Herbert V. Guenther. Reprinted by arrangement with Shambhala, Publications Inc., Boston, www.shambhala.com

**p.16:** Subhadassi (ed.), *FWBO New Poetry 1997*, Rising Fire, reprinted with kind permission of Thomas Jones.

**p.17 and p.34:**
Ted Hughes, *Hawk in the Rain*, Faber and Faber Ltd.

**p.26:** 'The desert has many teachings' by Mechtild of Magdeburg, trans. Jane Hirshfield from *Women in Praise of the Sacred* by Jane Hirshfield, editor. Copyright © 1994 by Jane Hirshfield. Reprinted by permission of HarperCollins Publishers, Inc.

**p.30:** reprinted from *The Kabir Book* translated by Robert Bly, Beacon Press, Boston 1977. Copyright 1977 Robert Bly. Used with his permission.

**p.33:** *The Selected Poetry of Rainer Maria Rilke* by Rainer Maria Rilke. Copyright © 1982 by Stephen Mitchell. Reprinted by permission of Random House, Inc.

**p.42:** Bhikkhu Nyanasobhana, *Landscapes of Wonder*, Wisdom Publications, Boston 1998.

**p.45:** *The Middle Length Discourses of the Buddha*, original translation by Bhikkhu Nanamoli, translated, edited, and revised by Bhikkhu Bodhi, Wisdom Publications, Boston 1995.

**p.47:** Lama Chonam and Sangye Khandro (trans.), *The Lives and*

*Liberation of Princess Mandarava*, Wisdom Publications, Boston 1998.

p.52: Jane Wilhelms (ed.), *Mother of Knowledge: The Enlightenment of Ye-shes mTsho-rgyal*, text by Nam-mkha'i snying-po, oral translation by Tarthang Tulku, Dharma Publishing 1983.

p.55: 'The Wild Swans at Coole', from W.B. Yeats, *Selected Poetry*, published by Pan Books in association with Macmillan, London 1974, seventh printing 1980. Reprinted with the permission of A.P. Watt Ltd. on behalf of Michael B. Yeats.

p.57: Excerpt from *Blue Pastures*, copyright © 1995, 1992, 1991 by Mary Oliver, reprinted by permission of Harcourt, Inc.


Every effort has been made to trace copyright in the following, but if any omission has been made please let us know in order that this may be acknowledged in the next edition.

p.9: by Owl Woman, trans. Frances Denmore, from *Women in Praise of the Sacred*, edited by Jane Hirshfield, HarperPerennial, first edition 1995.

p.38: from 'The Meeting at Silver Spring' in Garma C.C. Chang, *The Hundred Thousand Songs of Milarepa*, Shambhala, Boston and London, 1999, p.163

The Windhorse symbolizes the energy of the enlightened mind carrying the Three Jewels – the Buddha, the Dharma, and the Sangha – to all sentient beings. Buddhism is one of the fastest-growing spiritual traditions in the Western world. Throughout its 2,500-year history, it has always succeeded in adapting its mode of expression to suit whatever culture it has encountered.

WINDHORSE PUBLICATIONS aims to continue this tradition as Buddhism comes to the West. Today's Westerners are heirs to the entire Buddhist tradition, free to draw instruction and inspiration from all the many schools and branches. Windhorse publishes works by authors who not only understand the Buddhist tradition but are also familiar with Western culture and the Western mind. Manuscripts welcome.

For orders and catalogues contact

| WINDHORSE PUBLICATIONS 11 Park Road Birmingham B13 8AB UK | WINDHORSE BOOKS P.O. Box 574 Newtown NSW 2042 Australia | WEATHERHILL INC 41 Monroe Turnpike Trumbull CT 06611 USA |
|---|---|---|

Windhorse Publications is an arm of the FRIENDS OF THE WESTERN BUDDHIST ORDER, which has more than sixty centres on five continents. Through these centres, members of the Western Buddhist Order offer regular programmes of events for the general public and for more experienced students. These include meditation classes, public talks, study on Buddhist themes and texts, and 'bodywork' classes such as t'ai chi, yoga, and massage. The FWBO also runs several retreat centres and the Karuna Trust, a fund-raising charity that supports social welfare projects in the slums and villages of India. Many FWBO centres have residential spiritual communities and ethical businesses associated with them. Arts activities are encouraged too, as is the development of strong bonds of friendship between people who share the same ideals.

In this way the FWBO is developing a unique approach to Buddhism, not simply as a set of techniques, less still as an exotic cultural interest, but as a creatively directed way of life for people living in the modern world.

If you would like more information about the FWBO please visit our website at

| www.fwbo.org | or write to |
| London Buddhist Centre | Aryaloka |
| 51 Roman Road | Heartwood Circle |
| London | Newmarket |
| E2 0HU, UK | NH 03857, USA |

# ALSO FROM WINDHORSE

Compiled by Vidyadevi
REFLECTIONS ON SOLITUDE

Throughout the ages seekers after truth have spoken of the benefits of solitude for reflection, self-examination, and a deeper understanding of life.

This diverse and thoughtful selection of poetry and prose draws on the riches of Western literature as well as the wisdom of the Buddhist tradition, depicting the many delights and challenges of being alone.

Spend a little time with these reflections when life is crowding in on you and find some space...

*80 pages*
*ISBN 1 899579 28 1*
*£4.99/$9.95*

Sangharakshita
THE CALL OF THE FOREST
AND OTHER POEMS

Profound contemplation of nature and spiritual
vision feature prominently in this collection of
Sangharakshita's recent poems. Here we can see
how the practice of Buddhism combines with
the writing of poetry. Both require the cultivation of an intense sympathy with others, which
forms the basis of the essential Buddhist virtue of
loving-kindness.

*56 pages*
*ISBN 1 899579 24 9*
*£7.99/$15.95*

Sangharakshita
COMPLETE POEMS 1941-1994

Sangharakshita has dedicated himself to helping people transform their lives not only through his work as a Buddhist teacher but also through the medium of verse, for in his poetry he combines the sensitivity of the poet with the vision born of a life of contemplation and uncompromising spiritual practice.

Here we have the opportunity to listen to a unique voice and to be uplifted by the reflections of an extraordinary person and an accomplished teacher.

*528 pages, hardback*
*ISBN 0 904766 70 5*
*£17.99/$34.95*

Sir Edwin Arnold
THE LIGHT OF ASIA

This inspiring poem by Sir Edwin Arnold
(1832–1904), though written more than a
hundred years ago, retains the power to move us
in a way that no prose rendering of the life of the
Buddha can. We cannot but admire the courage,
determination, and self-sacrifice of the Indian
prince who, out of compassion, left his palace to
find a remedy for the sufferings of the world.

*192 pages, hardback, with glossary*
*ISBN 1 899579 19 2*
*£9.99/$19.95*

Sangharakshita
PEACE IS A FIRE

This collection of aphorisms, teachings, and poems by the pioneering Western Buddhist Sangharakshita offers instant inspiration to anyone who is ready to have their views challenged and their minds expanded.

The breadth of the author's thought is well represented in these sayings which range from art and literature, through sex and relationships, to philosophy and religion. His words point beyond themselves to Reality itself, to the freedom accessible to all who dare to change.

*160 pages, with photographs*
*ISBN 0 904766 84 5*
*£6.99/$13.95*

Sangharakshita

A STREAM OF STARS:
REFLECTIONS AND APHORISMS

This is a collection of aphorisms, poems, and writings by the eminent Western Buddhist teacher, Sangharakshita. Encompassing culture and society, relationships and the human condition, these incisive teachings illuminate many aspects of life.

With clarity, insight, and flashes of humour, Sangharakshita provokes us to thought and then to aspiration: an aspiration to true happiness and freedom.

*136 pages, with photographs*
*ISBN 1 899579 08 7*
*£6.99/$13.95*